masterpieces of style masterpieces of

masterpieces of style masterpieces of
masterpieces of style masterpieces of
masterpieces of style masterpieces of
masterpieces of style masterpieces of
masterpieces of style masterpieces of
masterpieces of style masterpieces of
masterpieces of style masterpieces of
masterpieces of style masterpieces of
masterpieces of style masterpieces of
masterpieces of style masterpieces of
masterpieces of style masterpieces of
masterpieces of style masterpieces of

masterpieces of style

VIGNALE

masterpieces of style

Giorgio Nada Editore Srl

Editorial manager
Leonardo Acerbi

Editorial
Giorgio Nada Editore

Translation
Neil Davenport

Graphic Design and layout
Sansai Zappini

Cover
Sansai Zappini

DESIGNED & MANUFACTURED IN ITALY

Giorgio Nada Editore
Via Claudio Treves, 15/17
I – 20090 VIMODRONE MI
Tel. +39 02 27301126
Fax +39 02 27301454
E-mail: info@giorgionadaeditore.it
http://www.giorgionadaeditore.it

Allo stesso indirizzo può essere richiesto il catalogo di tutte le opere pubblicate dalla Casa Editrice.

The catalogue of Giorgio Nada Editore publications is available on request at the above address.

Distribution:
Giunti Editore SpA
via Bolognese 165
I – 50139 FIRENZE
www.giunti.it

VIGNALE. Masterpieces of style
ISBN: 978-88-7911-721-0

Picture credits:
Archivio Giorgio Nada Editore/Franco Villani Collection and Novafoto-Sorlini
Archivio Quattroruote (Editoriale Domus)

The pictures shown in the following list are taken from "Ghia-Vignale. I capolavori dello Stile", Ruoteclassiche, Editoriale Domus, 2016

Pag. 4, 6-7, 8, 12, 15, 16. 17 (top), 18 (top), 19, 20, 22, 24-25, 26 (top), 28, 29, 34 (bottom), 35, 38, 40 (top), 41 (top), 42 (top), 44, 45, 49 (top), 50, 52, 54 (top), 56-57, 58, 59, 63 (bottom), 68-69, 70, 71, 82, 83, 85 (bottom), 86-87, 93, 98, 101 (top and bottom/right), 102 (top), 105, 111 (top), 112 (bottom), 118, 119, 120, 121, 128, 129, 136 (bottom), 138, 141-142, 153 (bottom), 161, 166, 172-173, 178, 179, 182-183, 191

VIGNALE

masterpieces of style

Texts edited by

Luciano Greggio

GIORGIO NADA EDITORE

350032 MO

Summary

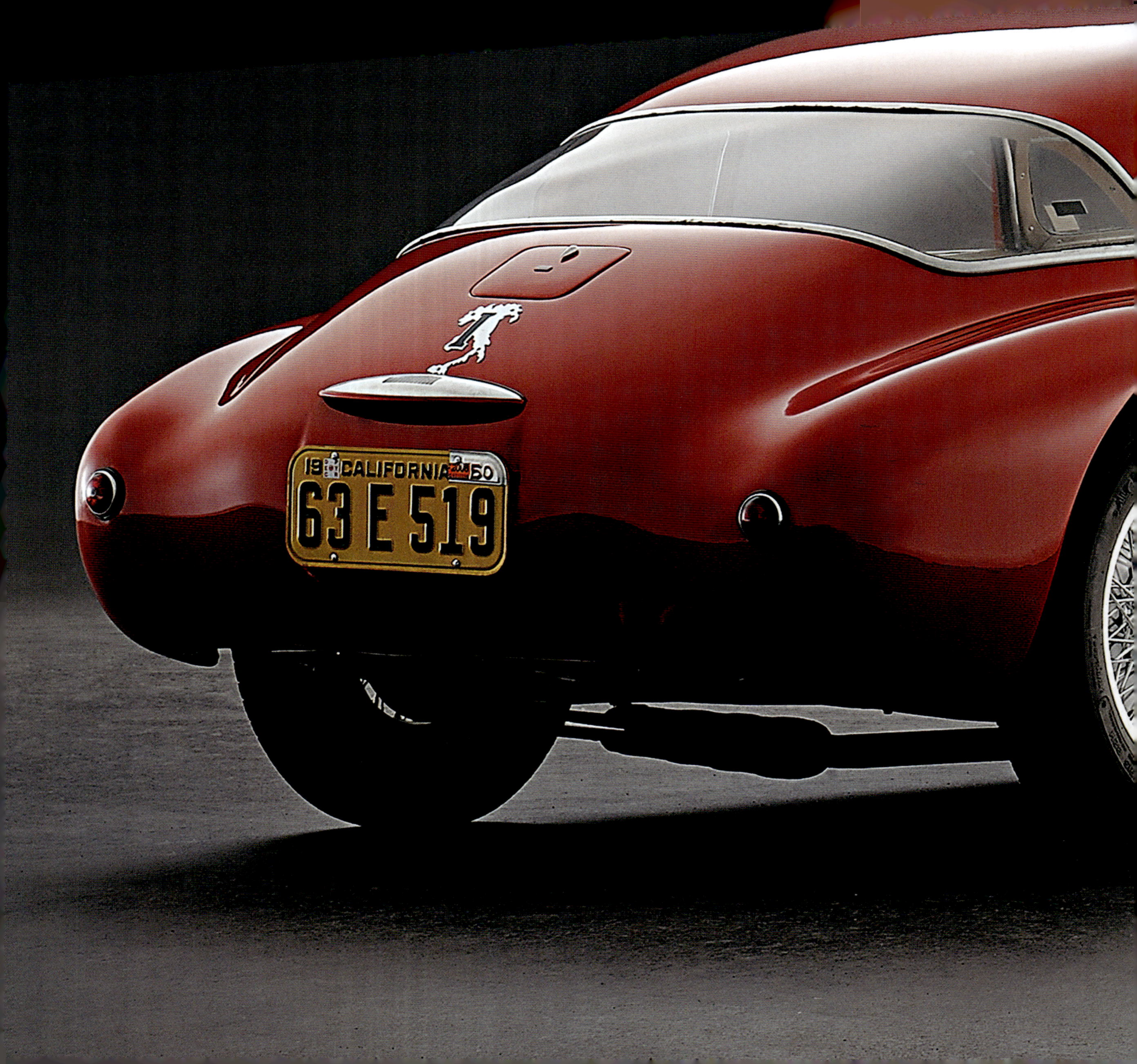
19 CALIFORNIA 50
63 E 519

THE ARTIFICIER OF THE FIRST FERRARIS

The progressive disappearance of coachbuilders specialising in the construction of custom bodies was a phenomenon that affected even the most well known names in the sector. Excluded from the market due to the epochal changes in public purchasing patterns, but also and above all to the evolution of the major manufacturers' successful diversification of their product range to include those niches formerly reserved for "special" models. Carrozzeria Vignale proved unable to escape this fate. Driven in the immediate post-war period by the talented and versatile Alfredo Vignale, the small Turin-based atelier was within a short space of time able to carve out space for itself within the variegated Italian coachbuilding world. It did so by distinguishing itself from the outset for flair and intelligence, alternating its own creations with profitable collaborations with leading manufacturers.

At the dawn of the 1950s, two episodes in particular influenced Vignale's fortunes: the first was the encounter with Giovanni Michelotti, the volcanic, ante litteram freelance stylist who found in the Turin coachbuilding firm the ideal setting in which to give free rein to his creativity and flair, designing models such as the Fiat 1400 Orchidea, the Abarth 204 A, the Cunningham C3, the unforgettable Démon Rouge based on the Fiat 8V, the BMW 507 and the various Triumph Heralds towards the end of that glorious decade.

The second was the meeting with Enzo Ferrari, who in Vignale found the man capable of interpreting to best effect the spirit of his racing barchettas and berlinettas. The Vignale-bodied Ferraris in fact represent a story within the story, one studded with unforgettable models based around the 166, 195, 212, 250 – the first model in this hugely successful and enduring series was signed off by Vignale –, 340 and 375 mechanicals. Cars capable of attracting attention at the principal motor shows of the period, while at the same time dominating in the most prestigious races, including the Mille Miglia.

A new factory and further prestigious commissions for Lancia, Fiat and Maserati came with the 1960s, but as the decade drew to a close, the beginning of the end could already be seen. It was in those years that Vignale crossed paths with Alejandro de Tomaso, a man who in those delicate circumstances conveyed the impression of being a "saviour".

An adventurer open to any compromise and blessed with an undoubtedly persuasive silver tongue, he cast his net in the direction of Vignale too. The Argentine, aware that production of the model on which he had pinned his hopes, the Pantera, could not rely on the modest facilities available to Ghia, homed in on the efficient new Vignale factory at Grugliasco that was capable assembling up to 16 car bodies a day. He came up with a scheme of having the factory produce the Pantera with Ghia badging and in the November of 1969 acquired a 90% shareholding in Vignale. The entire strategy then foundered due to the poor reputation earned by the first Panteras to be registered on the other side of the Atlantic, with Ford reacting by declining to import the car and to produce it in Italy.

Ironically, it was then to be Ford that revived the Vignale marque, but that is another story.

1946-1949
TALENTED PANEL BEATER

HAVING LEARNED THE SECRETS OF LENDING COMPLEX SHAPES TO SHEET ALUMINIUM FROM FRUA AND BOANO AND AFTER HEADING THE PANEL-BEATING DEPARTMENT AT STABILIMENTI FARINA, VIGNALE DECIDED TO SEEK HIS FORTUNE AND STRIKE OUT ON HIS OWN: THIS WAS ON THE 26TH OF OCTOBER, 1946.

In 1946, Alfredo Vignale (facing page) took the adventurous step of setting up his own coachbuilding firm in a modest workshop in Turin, where he put to good use the remarkable panel beating talent he had acquired from the 1930s at Stabilimenti Farina (bottom).

Alfredo Vignale was not part of that glorious first generation of Turin coachbuilders, although he had worked at a very young age at both Pinin Farina and Stabilimenti Farina, experiences that helped shape his initial aspirations and introduced him to the craft of panel beating. Born on the 15th of June, 1913, Alfredo learned the rudiments of the trade from those who in the early years of the last century had cultivated the art of transforming a bare rolling chassis into a magnificent motor car. In 1930, he came into contact with the new Pinin Farina firm, founded that year

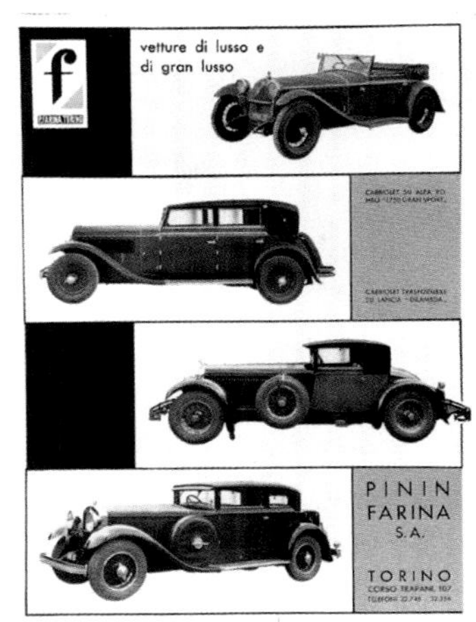

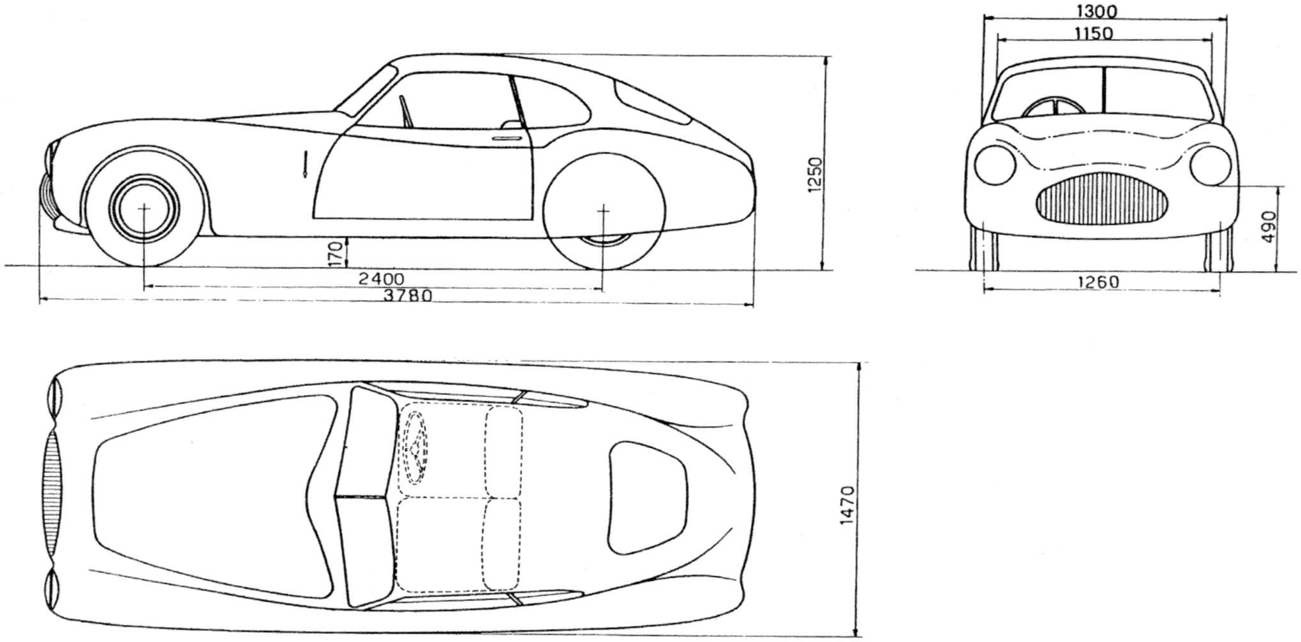

by Battista Farina who had broken away from the workshop of his elder brother Giovanni, the Stabilimenti Farina. Alfredo's ability in the modelling of sheet aluminium with the aid of an anvil, a mallet and hammers of various kinds, creating concave and convex forms, was noted and developed over time and his mastery of what was a particularly creative craft – the secrets of which were revealed to him by Mario Boano and Pietro Frua – allowed him in the second half of the 1930s to take over responsibility for the panel beating department of Giovanni Farina's firm, which at the time had a workforce of almost 1,000 and where his father Francesco and his brothers Eusebio and Guglielmo were already working. The young craftsman's wonderful manual skills and his untiring dedication to his work defined his professional profile but struggled to find adequate expression during the years of the Second World War. Alfredo's great dream, that of taking the courageous step of setting up his own company had to wait

One of the first drawings produced by Ing. Savonuzzi for the future Cisitalia 202 SC berlinetta. Savonuzzi himself, together with Alfredo Vignale, was to produce the executive designs for the magnificent 202 in the summer of 1946.

CISITALIA

COUPÉ BIPOSTO TIPO SPORT SPECIAL

until the immediate post-war years. Carrozzeria Vignale & C. was founded on the 26th of October 1946, a limited company (of which Alfredo became the managing director), based in Via Cigliano 29/31; with it was born the firm's rectangular logo featuring a blue ground with two small red triangles at the bottom. In the centre stood the towering Mole Antonelliana set within a large white V, the initial letter of the Vignale name.

Alfredo Vignale was not unprepared for design work, having, attended as a very young man a three-year evening course that was equivalent to a middle school education, during which he picked up the initial notions that allowed him to develop on a professional footing. At 17 years old in 1930, he had already acquired considerable experience as a panel beater at the Ferrero e Morandi workshop, from where, as mentioned, he moved to Pinin Farina, to the great temple recently consecrated to Italian coachbuilding. The modest workshop in Via Cigliano had a covered area of around 1,000 square metres and it was there at 33 years old the novice entrepreneur set about bodying sporadic rolling chassis produced by Fiat and Lancia, which were flanked by those constructed by Cisitalia, a new marque with which in 1946 Piero Dusio caressed the ephemeral dream of playing a significant role as a maker of sporting cars. It was actually Dusio who recognised the extraordinary talent of the panel beater Vignale in the modelling of the sheet metal for the 202 MM aerodynamic berlinetta, designed by Giovanni Savonuzzi for the 1947 Mille Miglia. That same year Alfredo had already drawn attention to himself with the successful rebodying of an accident damaged Fiat Topolino, the result earning the approval of Pinin Farina himself. For Vignale, 1947 represented a significant year in his approach to the sector and brought the Fiat 11 cabriolet that represented his official debut and was presented at the Concours d'Elegance at the Giardini Reali in Turin. This was followed by a two-seater Fiat 1500 cabriolet, a car exhibited that year at the Concours d'Elegance in the Boboli Gardens, Florence, and which was presented the following year at the European Grand Prix

The unmistakeable Carrozzeria Vignale badge, with the spire of the Mole Antonelliana in Turin above the letter V; below, the entrance to the first modest workshop housing the Vignale firm.

In 1947, Vignale presented this Fiat 1500 cabriolet (six cylinders, 1493 cc, 45 hp at 4400 rpm) at the Concours d'Elegance in Boboli Gardens in Florence. The car was distinguished by the long, continuous lines of its flanks.

of Style at Juan-les-Pins in France. The 31st edition of the Turin Motor Show was inaugurated in September 1948 at the trade fair grounds in Turin's Parco del Valentino, symbolising the rebirth of the Italian car industry in the post-war period. Vignale was present with a stand that featured side by side a berlinetta on a Fiat 1100 B chassis, another with Lancia Aprilia mechanicals and an Alfa Romeo 6C 2500 cabriolet.

One of the most daring designs in the history of Italian coachbuilding: the Cisitalia experimental berlinetta, created by Giovanni Savonuzzi and characterised by conspicuous tail fins that gave the car a particular appeal and dynamism. Left, the car raced by Piero Taruffi (No. 150) in the 1947 edition of the Mille Miglia; bottom, Taruffi again, paired with Domenico Rabbia, was to start the 1948 edition of the Brescian race with car number 7.

Early in 1947, Piero Dusio decided to entrust the coupé to Pinin Farina to improve the bodywork, making it more harmonious and sleeker. In this photo, a 202 B (1949-1950) again prepared by Vignale.

The first body to carry the Vignale badge was this Fiat 1100 cabriolet (straight-four, 1089 cc, 32 hp at 4400 rpm) built in 1947 and adopting the conventional engineering shared by the other Italian coachbuilders of the immediate post-war period. The car was presented at the Concours d'Elegance in Turin's Giardini Reali.

Above, another photo of the Fiat 6C 1500 cabriolet that "triumphed" in the Florence Concours d'Elegance. Among the features of this elegant design was the line of the door opening and the rear wheel cover release mechanism, actuated by a button. Below, again in the open car field, Vignale also tackled the fascinating Cisitalia 202 cabriolet theme, producing a number of examples on commission, with detail variations with respect to the Pinin Farina model. Specifically, the eye-catching chrome trim running along the flanks.

Above, at the 1948 Turin Motor Show, Alfredo Vignale exhibited this elegant two-door saloon presented as the Vittoria and based on the Lancia Aprilia chassis (V4, 1486 cc engine producing 48 hp at 4300 rpm). The large, well-modelled bumper was an unmistakeable feature of Vignale's early creations and acquired a significant aesthetic value in the overall composition of the car.
Left, Vignale could hardly not tackle one of the classic cars of the period either side of the Second World War: the Alfa Romeo 6C 2500, the rather too sober lines of his design being only partially compensated by the luminous upper body.

Above, Vignale participated in the 1948 Turin Motor Show for the first time with a two-door saloon body on a Fiat 1100 B chassis (with a 35 hp engine), the front end of which featured an elegant V-shaped front grille, inspired by that of the Fiat production model.
Below, another example of attractive front end modelling distinguished this two-door saloon based on Lancia Aprilia mechanicals, one of the cars most popular with both the general public at the motor shows and the specialist press.
This car, of which a four-door version was also produced, was entered in the Concours d'Elegance at the Venice Lido in 1949.

1950-1954

THE ENCOUNTER WITH MICHELOTTI

THE COLLABORATION WITH THE TALENTED DESIGNER LED TO THE PRODUCTION OF MORE THAN A THOUSAND SKETCHES, FROM WHICH EMERGED A NUMBER OF MASTERPIECES, DISTINGUISHED BY A PERFECT BALANCE OF CRAFT AND STYLISTIC INNOVATION. AMONG THE SPORTS COUPÉS WERE THE ABARTH 204 A AND THE CUNNINGHAM C3.

Facing page, Alfredo established a close personal and professional relationship with the stylist Giovanni Michelotti (on the right in the photo) who had also gained invaluable experience at Stabilimenti Farina. That partnership was to produce a number of great successes for the company. Among the most important commissions obtained by Vignale was the initial production in a limited series of bodywork for the Cisitalia 202 B of 1949, a model that in that period was also to enjoy a degree of success in racing.

In 1949, Alfredo's feverish proposal of new stylistic interpretations began to benefit from the collaboration with Giovanni Michelotti (also born in Turin, in 1921), who had left his position as a draughtsman at Stabilimenti Farina and then Allemano in order to establish himself as a freelance designer. He worked intensively as a consultant for half a dozen coachbuilders, but especially with Vignale, for whom the young stylist produced more than a thousand sketches, bringing a gust of pioneering fresh air to the world of Italian coachbuilding.

The first major commission gained by Vignale was for the limited series production in 1949 of bodywork for the Cisitalia 202 B, of which Pinin Farina had built the first examples. This commission permitted the fledgling entrepreneur to emerge from an initial heroic period in which he had turned to producing bicycle mudguards, aluminium pans and ice-boxes before he could finally devote himself to producing custom car bodies. In what was to be his true vocation he combined a remarkable degree of manual skill with the inspired sophistication of the experienced craftsman. Evidence of this rapid evolutionary process was seen in the spring of 1950, when Alfredo clothed the chassis of the brand-new Fiat 1400 with the Orchidea bodywork featuring integral glazing, a car that was displayed at the Turin Motor Show (brought forward to the spring that year),

The Vignale stand at the 1950 Turin Motor Show, held in the spring that year, which featured the Orchidea (in the foreground), flanked by a Fiat 1500 E and a Fiat 1100 E in two- and four-door forms.

The 1951 Turin Motor Show saw the launch of the Abarth 205 A, closely related to the earlier 204 A. The ovoid air vents and the shapely radiator grille were to become over the years distinguishing features of the Carrozzeria Vignale.

together with a further six models. This line-up also saw Vignale present on the Abarth stand with the splendid 204 A berlinetta (with Fiat-Cisitalia mechanicals including the 1100 cc engine producing 83 hp). Low and sleek, the model was distinguished by the three small air vents on the flanks that subsequently became unmistakable styling motifs of Vignale's sporting cars. The other car that appeared at the Turin Show that year was the Packard Eight cabriolet, an enormous, solemn vehicle (powered by a 4.7-litre straight-eight producing 139 hp), with a radiator grille inspired by that of the production model. The construction of a car body, composed of a shell with a frame of narrow-gauge steel tubes clothed with panels in sheet aluminium, always saw Alfredo playing a key role in the workshop where the panels took shape thanks to the skills

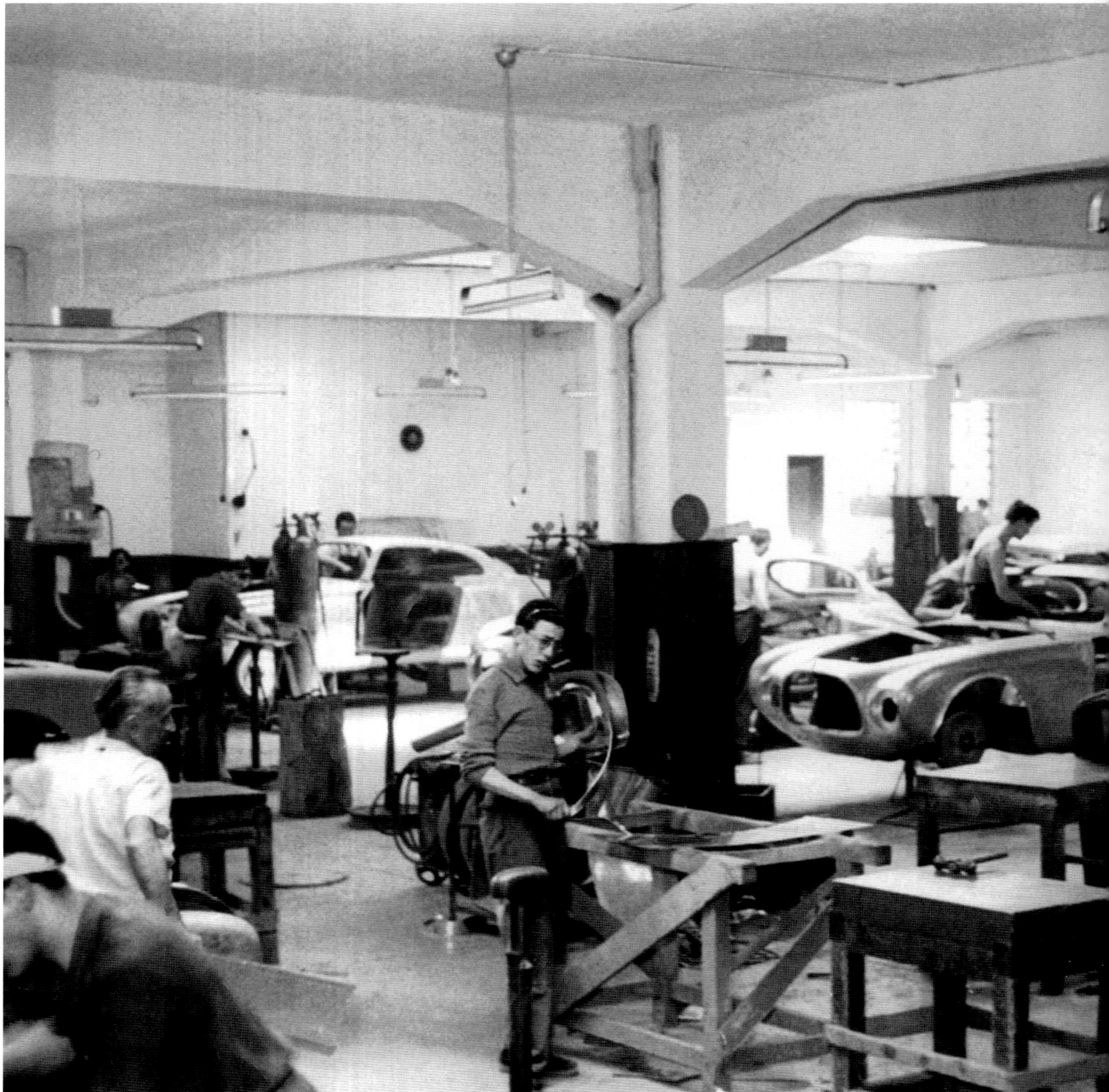

of the panel beaters, a craft in which Vignale had shone for years, building up a remarkable reputation. In contrast with the approach adopted in the Fifties and Sixties by the majority of Italian coachbuilders focusing on the production of small batches of cars, Alfredo clung to the original craft-based configuration of his business which allowed him to work on the basis of one-off pieces or at most a dozen examples of the same design; in any case, each of those examples would have differed with respect to the others in certain personal details, all of which helped enhance his reputation as an exclusive creator. Vignale distinguished himself in this period with an unbridled design personality deriving from his youthful experience as a panel beater and his exceptional ability in transferring to sheet aluminium shapes at times traced on the floor in chalk. In his singular role as a coachbuilder inspired by strongly innovative spirit, Vignale expressed himself with cars that were at times sober, but at others complex and extravagant. His creations, which frequently swam against the tide of the prevailing stylistic canons of the period, had a great

An overview of the Vignale workshop in the early Fifties: the car bodies were fully hand-built, relying on the skill of the *magnin*, as the panelbeaters were known in the Piedmont dialect. Wood and metal were the materials of choice.

The debut of the Fiat 1100/103 at the 1953 Geneva Motor Show represented for Vignale a precious opportunity to give free rein to his creativity, underpinned by the consolidated mechanicals. Within a few years, the Vignale-Michelotti pairing gave rise to the Antibes coupé, characterised by a prominent radiator grille and an inevitable series of "giardinetta" station wagons of great appeal and elegance.

influence on Giovanni Michelotti, whose occasionally excessive imagination found an ideal foil in Alfredo's impeccable craftsmanship. Their car bodies were all splendid testimony to a maniacal attention to detail in which there was always an innovative stylistic message informed by pure functionality. Significant examples included the chrome-plated air vents of diverse shapes (ovals, rectangles, arrow-heads...) fitted along the sides of the bonnet or the sills, the large triangular slots behind the front wheel arches designed to improve brake cooling and the eccentric positioning of the chrome-plated rear lighting clusters set into the wings. Another characteristic feature was that of setting the headlights in the front panel, either side of the radiator grill, buried in the long, forward thrusting wings. Within this constant stream of new forms emerged the stunning use of chrome-plated trim graphics that proved capable of expressing an unusual and at times provocative design idiom. Vignale's attention to foreign markets was almost immediately focused on the Anglo-Saxon world, starting with the proposal in 1951 for the new Riley Pathfinder powered by a 2.5-litre engine (102 hp). The firm's work

It was inevitable that in the early Fifties Vignale too would take an interest in the transatlantic trends and the enormous potential of that market. The 808 XF coupé (1953) was one model that came out of this interest, a car that Cisitalia offered to Henry Ford with a view to possible mass production although nothing came of the project, another was the Bill Frick Special cabriolet (1953), a number of examples of which were prepared on Cadillac mechanicals.

for the American Cunningham marque resulted in the Continental C3 of 1952, perhaps one of the most elegant coupés of the post-war years. The dynamic, perceptive presence of Giovanni Michelotti alongside Vignale was decisive in projecting the Via Cigliano-based company into the ranks of the most famous international coachbuilders. The designer's creative intuition harmonized with the masterful skills of the craftsman and both expressed themselves through forms of great originality; there were cars of great and at times raffish appeal, with a distinct personality that earned widespread approval among a clientele that included King Baudouin of Belgium for whom an exclusive coupé was created in 1955 on the Aston Martin DB2/4 rolling chassis.

The Fiat 1400 Orchidea (straight-four, 1395 cc, 44 hp at 4400 rpm) was exhibited successfully by Vignale at the Geneva Motor Show in 1950 and proposed elegant shapes and a very airy interior, distinguished by a large wrap-around rear screen integrated with the sloping line of the tail.

Facing page, top, the multi-faceted creativity of Giovanni Michelotti found full expression in 1950 in this Fiat 1400 Primula coupé too, a car characterised by an unusual elliptical grille and attractive sweeping flanks with a slight kick to the shapely rear wing. This model was very popular with the public and was also offered in cabriolet form. Below, a sensation was caused on the Packard stand at the 1950 Turin Motor Show by this imposed Eight cabriolet (straight-eight, 4719 cc, 139 hp at 3600 rpm), finished in light blue and distinguished by a monumental grille inspired by that of the production model. It remained a one-off, but aroused considerable interest in the coachbuilding world.

PIRELLI

PACKARD

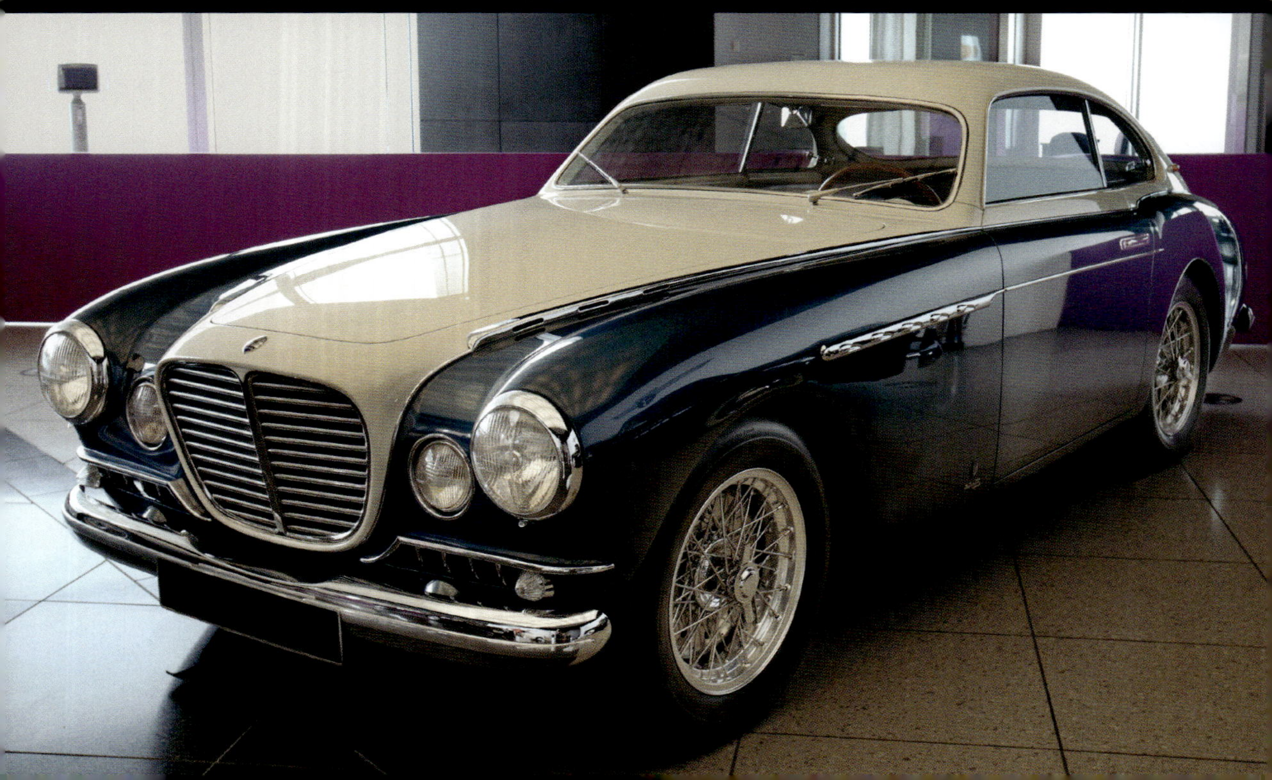

Facing page, another of Vignale staples in those fabulous Fifties was two-tone paintwork capable of exalting shapes and volumes. A valid example in this sense is offered by the Maserati A6G 2000 from 1950, which in the two-tone livery was particularly sleek, especially the flanks. The radiator grille was notable elegant, which the used of chrome trim was well judged.

Top, another car from 1950 bodied on a Lancia Aurelia rolling chassis – an extraordinary source of inspiration for Vignale too – was the Erminia, named after the client who commissioned it (Erminio Macario). This sumptuous coupé offered among other features an original interpretation of the classic Aurelia grille, of reduced dimensions and set further forwards.

23895 NO

Aurelia
NO 2
3895

The Vignale-Michelotti pairing was to give rise in the early Fifties to a small batch of elegant and attractive coupés based on the Lancia Aurelia. In the photos on these two pages, one of the first examples characterised by an interesting rereading of the Lancia grille, two-tone bodywork and a wrap-around rear screen.

Created by Carlo Abarth on a box-section chassis (a configuration beloved of the manufacturer) and powered by a Cisitalia engine displacing 1089 cc (83 hp at 6000 rpm), the 204 A presented an elegant body, skilfully prepared on the basis of sketch by Michelotti. The competition career of the 204 berlinetta began on the 26th of March 1950 in the second edition of the Coppa Intereuropa: entered by the Abarth team and driven by Guido Scagliarini, it won its class.

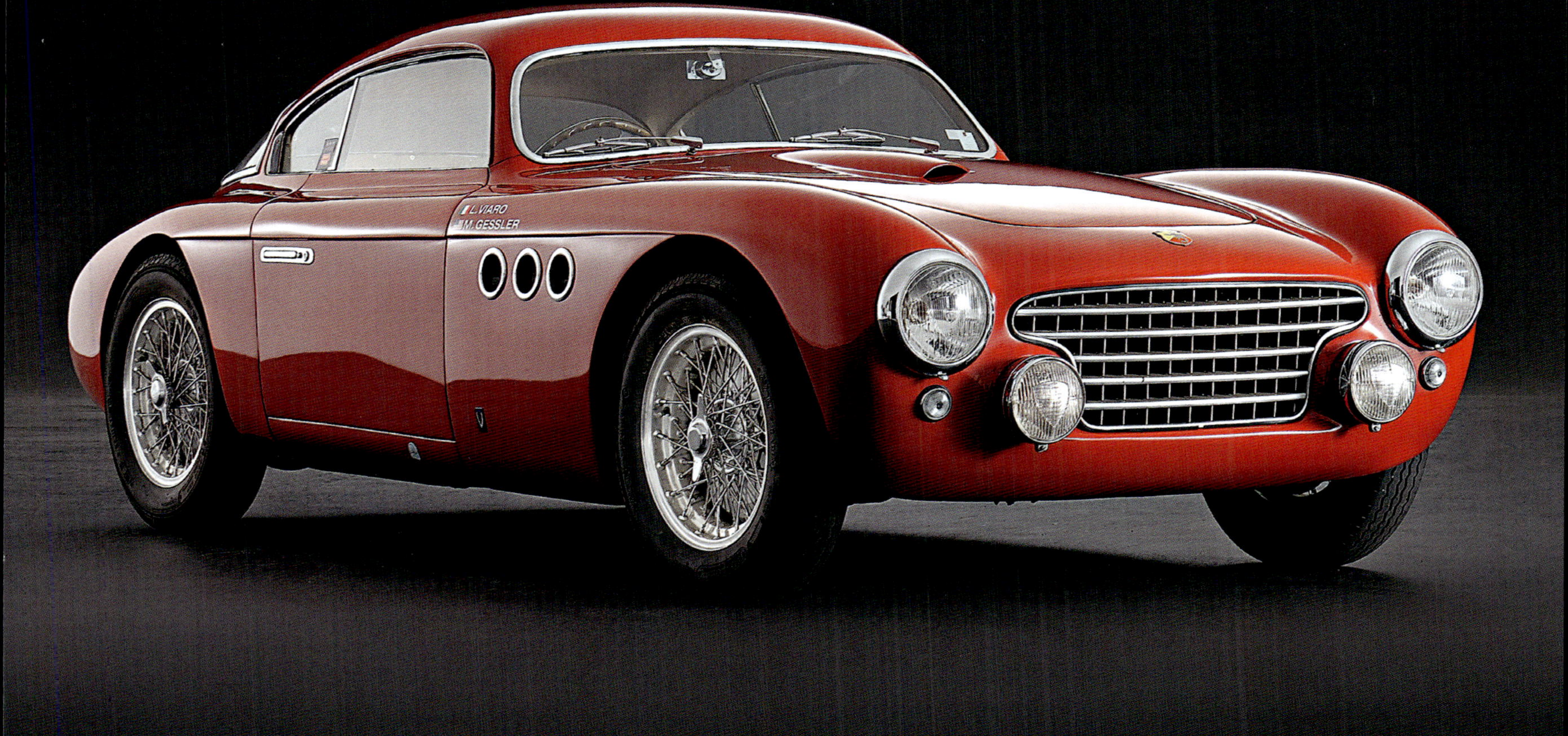
L. VIARO
M. GESSLER

CALIFORNIA
63 E 519
L. VIARO
M. GESSLER

Built around the combination of the 8C 2900 A chassis and the 4495 cc V12 engine fuelled by triple carburettors (220 hp at 5500 rpm), the Alfa Romeo 412 (built between 1939 and 1949) participated in sports car races thanks to a number of clients. Among them was the driver Felice Bonetto who had Vignale body with two-seater racing version to the designs of his nephew Rodolfo Bonetto. He drove this original car in the 1951 Mille Miglia (28-29 April), finishing in 6th place overall after 13:49.35 hours of racing.

Vignale constructed the bodies for a batch of Cunningham C3s (a total of nine examples) with tubular chassis and Chrysler hemi engines (V8, 5426 cc, 270 hp). Commissioned in 1952 by Briggs Swift Cunningham – a well-known American driver and constructor – the model enjoyed a moment of great popularity in the US. In this case too, the two-tone paintwork adds something extra, but also of note are the elliptical front grille, notably dished behind the headlights, and the massive chrome-plated front bumper.

DUNLOP RACING

The exceptional creativity of Giovanni Michelotti was fully expressed in this cabriolet based on the Lancia Aurelia B52 (V6, 1991 cc, 70 hp at 4800 rpm), prepared by Vignale in 1952. Coachbuilt examples of the Aurelia were in that period the most admired and sought-after cars among a well-informed European clientele, as shown by the sumptuous coupé seen below, characterised by a particularly elaborate front-end design.

Michelotti's creative drive and the great talent of Vignale as a panel beater gave rise in 1953 to this Alfa Romeo 1900 Sprint (straight-four, 1884 cc, 100 hp at 5500 rpm), a highly original coupé that stood out among the other cars of the era based on the same rolling chassis.

The racing two-seater built by Vignale in 1953 on the Maserati A6 GCS rolling chassis (twin-cam straight-six, 1978 cc, 170 hp at 7300 rpm) aroused discordant opinions due to the exhaust pipes on the left-hand side that strongly characterised the styling of the car. Nonetheless, in that period Vignale produced a number of excellent styling exercises on the "barchetta" theme.

Left, another racing car, the OSCA MTt4 1100 built in 1952 for Gianni Balzarini. This car, distinguished by scooped flanks and a front end that recalled that of the contemporary Ferrari 340 Mexico, participated in the 1953 Mille Miglia, as seen in this rare colour photo by Alberto Sorlini.

One of the most striking cars bodied by Vignale in the early Fifties was the Fiat 8V (chassis No. 00052) bodied in 1953, which featured faired headlights, a close-coupled upper body, a fastback tail and, once again, a two-tone finish.

Vignale was present at the 1953 Turin Motor Show with a coupé (above) based on the Fiat 1100/103 (1089 cc, 36 hp) with bodywork by Michelotti featuring an elaborate grille, either side of which were inset headlight. There was also an interesting one-off interpretation in 1954 of the coupé theme, the lines of which had a strong forwards projection (facing page, top). That same year Vignale launched a limited series production of the 1100 Charmant coupé based on both the normal Fiat 1100/103 mechanicals and on the TV (Turismo Veloce) version.

SARPOM
O. M.
EMANUEL

1950-1954
THE ADVENTURE WITH THE ROSSE

THE OPPORTUNITY TO BODY THE PRESTIGIOUS ROLLING CHASSIS FROM MARANELLO OPENED THE WAY FOR TRIUMPHANT SUCCESS IN RACING TOO. A PAIRING THAT GAVE RISE TO GTS OF GREAT ELEGANCE WITH STYLING MOTIFS OF GREAT EFFECT, THAT WON OVER DRIVERS, SOVEREIGNS AND FILM STARS ALIKE.

Facing page. In the early Fifties, Franco Cornacchia (in the photo on the right), founder of the Scuderia Guastalla, a good driver and a trustee of Ferrari, was the link between the still newly formed Maranello manufacturer and Alfredo Vignale. This photo shows Cornacchia talking to the driver Emilio Romano during scrutineering ahead of the 1951 Mille Miglia.

Just like Vignale, Enzo Ferrari had founded his small factory at Maranello in 1946 and had come into contact with the Turin panel beater through Franco Cornacchia, a well-known driver and owner of the Scuderia Guastalla as well as the Milan representative of the Prancing Horse marque. The two constructors shared certain personal characteristic, with both being known for their extreme dedication to their work and for their conviction that they were the sole arbiters capable of making decisions that concerned their companies. The agreement between them was reached when Ferrari entrusted his rolling chassis to Touring of Milan, which in effect made a vital contribution to creating the celebrated image of the Italian 12-cylinder cars in the worlds of motor racing and high society. However, the Maranello constructor, allergic to long-term commitments, was on the look out not for a new coachbuilder, but rather a true artist, one with a wealth of skill but also daring intuitions, capable of undertaking with the same enthusiasm the rebodying of an accident-damaged car and the construction from scratch of an eccentric body for one of the most picturesque characters of the era.

The first dazzling car carrying the Prancing Horse badge to be bodied in Via Cigliano was the 166 MM berlinetta (chassis No. 0062 MM) built

in 1950 for Cornacchia, a model created by the famous Vignale-Michelotti pairing, was to be recognised in the years to come as the inspiration for a great number of cars that have earned a place in Italian automotive history. It was a moment of great euphoria between the two, their relationship soon being consolidated: in the case of a sketch presented by Michelotti that did not meet with the complete approval of the versatile coachbuilder, on the strength of his great experience Vignale himself would intervene to confer simpler and at times less controversial modelling. The Ferraris designed by Michelotti and bodied by Vignale (less than 160 examples) were little or greatly different to one another, but all were identified by those

Here is Franco Cornacchia in the 212 Export berlinetta bodied by Vignale with which he disputed the 1951 Mille Miglia, paired with Guido Mariani. The two took the elegant coupé through to the finish in 17th place overall, 8th in the over two-litre Sport and Group A category and 6th in class.

The Argentinian driver Froilán González seen in front of the Vignale premises in 1951 ready to pick up his Ferrari 166 MM (chassis No. 0038 M), surrounded by some of the workers. The car was rebodied on the basis of an earlier Touring barchetta.
Below, a 195 Inter in an official Vignale advertisement.

spontaneous forms that in the coachbuilding environment preceded the hand-building phase in limited numbers before passing to the subsequent stage that spread rapidly with the family look phenomenon.

Among the models of exceptional elegance created in the early Fifties were the Ferrari 212 Export spider (chassis No. 0090 E), a splendid Vignale interpretation of the two-seater barchetta theme that made its debut at the 1951 Geneva Motor Show and was delivered on the 12th of March to Umberto Marzotto of the famous Valdagno dynasty. In that car, Vignale expressed the best of the Italian styling school, with a long prominent body, subtly modelled flanks, a very small windscreen and an almost absolute absence of chrome trim, a choice intended to valorize the beauty of the shapes.

The close relationship that was created in this period between the avant-garde stylist and the panel beater led to further splendid cars, sculpted like rare *objets d'art* that found favour with European nobility, famous sportsmen and well-known show business celebrities.

405

Ferrari
Ferrari
PIRELLI
CORSA

Facing page, the Ferrari 340 America bodied by Vignale in 1951 on chassis No. 0082A which won the Mille Miglia that year (28-29 April) with the Villoresi-Cassani crew, covering the 1,564 of the race at an average speed of 121.822 kph, despite a violent crash of which it shows the signs.
Below, Luigi Chinetti, the legendary Ferrari importer to the United States, at the wheel of the 340 America (chassis No. 1040 A).

Right, the sober coupé based around 212 E mechanicals (chassis No. 02111), bodied in 1952 for Gianni Agnelli, already a faithful and "particular" client of the Maranello marque.

Among the extraordinary examples of cars from Maranello bodied by Vignale were the 195 Inter (chassis No. 095S) displayed at the 1951 Turin Motor Show, the 212 Export (chassis No. 0111 ES), built in 1951 and presented as a one-off at the Concours d'Elegance de Bagatelle 1989, the stunning yellow 340 America spider (chassis No. 0140 A) ordered by Luigi Chinetti – Ferrari's New York importer – and since then always owned by a series of US clients, the 225 S (chassis No. 0154 ED) with which Vittorio Marzotto won the Monte Carlo Grand Prix in 1952 (the race being run for sports cars that year), the 212 Export coupé (chassis No. 0170 ET) from 1952, used that year in the Mille Miglia, the Trieste-Opicina, the Aosta-Gran San Bernardo and the Vittorio Veneto-Cansiglio, the winner of its class in the Italian national championship.

To these can be added the 195 Inter (chassis No. 0181 EL), originally owned by the actress Anna Magnani, the 125 S spider (chassis No. 182 ED), with which Paolo Marzotto won the 1952 Coppa d'Oro delle Dolomiti, the Giro delle Calabrie and the Circuito di Senigallia, the extremely elegant 212 Inter coupé (chassis No. 0211 EL) for Gianni Agnelli, the fantastic 340 Mexico coupé (chassis No. 0226 AT), driven in the November of 1952

CON
BO
16722

Facing page, loading the Ferrari 340 Mexicos aboard the Constitution ahead of the 1952 Carrera Panamericana. Vignale bodied three berlinettas on chassis Nos. 0222 AT (Villoresi-Cornacchia), 0224 AT (Chinetti-Lucas) and 0226 AT (Ascari-Scotuzzi) as well as a spider on chassis No. 0228 AT. That year victory had to be ceded to the Mercedes-Benz 300 SLs of Kling and Lang, respectively first and second. Above, one of the three berlinettas is featured in official Vignale promotional material.

by Ascari and Scotuzzi in the Carrera Panamericana, the 250 MM (chassis No. 0260 MM), delivered in March 1953 to Luigi Chinetti on behalf of a Californian client and the 375 American (chassis No. 327 AL), displayed at the Geneva and New York Motor Shows in 1954 and which has never left the United States since.

In 1953, Vignale bodied six Ferrari 166, ten 250 MM and five 340 MM rolling chassis with barchetta bodywork, testimony to the overwhelming success of these lightweight cars among clients with a clear sporting vocation. The last Ferrari bodied by Vignale was the 330 GT 2+2 from 1968 (chassis No. 7963), built at the behest of Luigi Chinetti for the US market, a kind of extravagant station wagon with a remarkable rear overhang, exhibited at the Turin Motor Show that opened on the 30th of October that year.

The Ferraris bodied by Vignale frequently played a decisive role in the races in which the Scuderia participated, for example the 212 Inters

Right, the Ferrari 340 MM Vignale barchetta (No. 0280 AM) of Count Giannino Marzotto and Marco Crosara about to cross the finishing line victorious in the 1953 Mille Miglia 1953 at an average speed of over 142 kph. Below, another barchetta from the Prancing Horse, the 250 MM (No. 0274 MM) showing strong stylistic affinities with the 340, demonstrating how Vignale had succeeded in finding an appropriate stylistic motif for the Ferrari sports cars of the period.

in the 1951 Carrera Panamericana and the 212 Exports, 250 S and 340 Mexico that competed successfully in the 1952 and 1953 editions of the race, along with the carts that triumphed in the Mille Miglia in 1951, 1952 and 1953. In the successful 1953 season, Vignale exhibited its reinterpretation of the famous MM racing berlinetta based around Ferrari 166, 250 and 340 mechanicals. This last version triumphed in its debut race, the Giro di Sicilia with the Villoresi-Cassani pairing and two weeks later won the Mille Miglia in the hands of Giannino Marzotto and Marco Crosara, a race valid for the new World Championship for Sports Cars. The two-litre 166 MM Vignale-bodied barchetta competed that year in the Giro di Sicilia with Sterzi and Pirovano, the Mille Miglia (Sterzi-Rossi) and in August in the Pescara 12 Hours (Sterzi-Cortese).

Facing page, Giampaolo Valletti and Alessandro Gaboardi salute the public just before descending the starting ramp at the 1956 Mille Miglia at the wheel of their 166/MM 53 (No. 0264 M) which they were unable to nurse to the finish.

The line drawing in profile of the 1954 Ferrari 250 GT Europa with the Ferrari and Vignale badges given equal standing. Below, the 225 S coupé (No. 0070 E) of Giovanni Brinci and Dorando Malinconi who took part in the 1955 Mille Miglia but had to retire early in the race.

526

181443 RA

RA·18
1443
I

Vignale's first contacts with 12-cylinder Ferraris were restricted to the rebodying of a number of Touring barchettas that had been badly damaged or to satisfy the whims of individual clients who wanted an exclusive body. The example seen here, identified with chassis No. 045 S, was one of the first 166 Inters to originally be fitted with a Vignale body. It was delivered on the 13th of October 1950 to the Milanese dealer Franco Cornacchia. Eight 166 Inters were bodied by Vignale (not rebodied).

Left, the T-shaped radiator grille and the large "superpanoramico" wrap-around rear screen conceived by Vignale for the Fiat 1400 Orchidea displayed at the 1950 Geneva Motor Show clearly inspired the Ferrari 166 Inter bodied at the end of the summer in 1950 on chassis No. 0065 S. Below, the 1951 Paris Motor Show saw this Ferrari 212 Inter bodied as a barchetta by Vignale on chassis No. 0135 E (V12, 2563 cc, 170 hp at 6500 rpm).

Facing page, on the 15th of April 1951, Gigi Villoresi won the GT category of the 3rd edition of the Coppa Intereuropa at Monza driving a Ferrari-Vignale 212 MM berlinetta (V12, 2563 cc, 220 hp at 7000 rpm).
Below, this elegant cabriolet was one of first creations by Vignale in 1951 on the 212 Inter chassis. The same bodywork was also offered with the mechanicals from the 212 Export, the engine being fitted with three Weber 36 DCL3 carburettors (220 hp).

126

The Ferrari 212 Export (chassis number 0080 E) built by Vignale in 1951 for Prince Vittorio Massimo di Roccasecca, one of the coachbuilder's best clients in this period.
On the facing page, Ferraris and more on the Vignale stand at the 1951 Turin Motor Show.

VIGNALE

Bemberg!
POLVERI EFFERVESCENTI
Baratti
SACEN
AUTO-CARROZZERIA
405

Facing page, at the last checkpoint in the 1951 Mille Miglia, the Ferrari 340 America (No. 0082 A) of Gigi Villoresi and Pasquale Cassani carries the unmistakeable "battle scars". They were not to prevent the car continuing on to Brescia and glory.
Right, Alberico Cacciari and Yvette Simon also participated in that edition of the race aboard a spectacular 166 MM Vignale spider (No. 0072 E) which they drove to 90th place overall.

The original two-tone paint finish introduced by Vignale in the Fifties was used on the Ferrari 212 Export with chassis No. 0111 ES from 1951 that in late November was delivered to Rome. In September 1952 it competed in the Bari Grand Prix and in 1953 in the Coppa Intereuropa.

As usual, a two-tone livery, a generous quadrangular grille, emphasised by the massive bumper, and the usual sober, elegant forms distinguished this 195 Inter (chassis No. 0099 S), also built in 1951.

The Ferrari barchetta in its simplest, purist form. Sleek lines of an extraordinary appeal and rigour characterise this spider based around 212 Inter mechanicals, also from 1951. Once again, the two-tone bodywork contributes to the elegance of the model.

VI·2
0824

Completed at Vignale on the 12th of March 1951, the spider bodywork on the Ferrari 212 Export chassis No. 0090 E was commissioned by Umberto Marzotto and then exported to the United States and registered to Donald Beatty in California. It then passed into the hands of Swedish collector Thomas A. Oleson before being exported to the USA once again. It was restored in 1989 in order to participate in the 1990 Mille Miglia revival with race number 296.

A magnificent body realised in 1952 on the Ferrari 212 Inter chassis No. 0211 EL was specially commissioned by Gianni Agnelli and featured a very original front end, with the headlights incorporated into the elliptical grille and the prominent tips of the wings.

There was an unusual front end to the 212 Inter berlinetta (chassis No. 0271) in which the bumper took the form of a central element placed below the radiator grille, along with two chrome quarter bumpers wrapping around the tips of the front wings. The car was displayed at the 1953 Geneva Motor Show and then shipped to the United States.

Scrutineering is in full swing ahead of the 1952 Mille Miglia. Apart from the Fiat Topolino that can be seen top left, all the other cars in the parc fermé were benefitted from the flair of the Carrozzeria Vignale, evidence of just how prolific was the relationship between the Turin coachbuilder and the firm from Maranello in those magnificent early Fifties.

603
610
611
533

611
611
W59°4999

The Vignale-bodied Ferraris appeared regularly in the Mille Miglia roll of honour, including the 1952 edition won by the Bracco-Rolfo pairing with the 250 S (chassis No. 0156 ET) on its first outing with the three-litre engine when it got the better of the Mercedes-Benz 300 SL of Karl Kling, beaten into second place. That stunning debut baptised an entire generation of Ferrari 250 GTs, nourishing the extraordinary reputation of the Prancing Horse in the GT category.
On these pages, the start and the glorious finish of that very wet Mille Miglia; in the midst of a truly legendary race, one of the highpoints of the long career of Giovanni Bracco.

A WÜHRER
MANELI
533

Facing page, as well as the 250 S of the winners Bracco and Rolfo, there was a gaggle of Ferraris by Vignale at the start of the 1952 Mille Miglia. Among the berlinettas was No. 533, a 166 MM (No. 0164 ED) driven by Bordoni and "Geronimo" to 10th place overall, just behind the twin car No. 537 (chassis No. 0152 EL) of Antonio Brivio Sforza and Pasquale Cassani, winners of their class. Caraceni and Meloni in their 225 S (No. 0170 ET) had a less successful race, being forced to retire early on.

Other Vignale berlinettas at the start of that 1952 Mille Miglia included No. 559, the 195 Inter (chassis No. 0147 E) of Sbraci and Giudici, retired,
and No. 603, the 212 Export (chassis No. 0178 ED) which also retired.
Facing page, the same fate awaited other barchettas such as No. 606, the 225 S of Bornigia and Bornigia and No. 614, the 340 America (No. 0196 A) of Taruffi-Vandelli.

606
606
PIRELLI
PIRELLI

614
614
CORSA

615
615

AUTOMOBILE CLUB
BRESCIA
Club
Mille Miglia
622

Just a minute after the departure of Taruffi's Ferrari, another 225 S barchetta descended the ramp, No. 615 (chassis No. 0172 ET) driven by Paolo Marzotto and Marino Marini (retired). The "veteran" Clemente Biondetti instead started at 6:22 aboard yet another 225 S, raced together with Giorgio Ercoli but not through to the finish.

Another Marzotto, Vittorio, makes his way between the crowds lining either side of the road in Brescia's Piazza della Vittoria, in his 225 S (No. 0154 ED), partnered by Otello Marchetto. They were also out of luck.

The Ferrari 212 Inter was bodied by Vignale in twin examples in the summer of 1951 on chassis 0161 EL and 0163 EL to participate in November in the Carrera Panamericana with the Chinetti-Taruffi and Ascari-Villoresi crews. They dominated the race, finishing first and second overall at Ciudad Juárez. This success was replicated in 1952-53 by another example, seen here, built on chassis No. 0292 MM, sent by Ferrari to Vignale on the 23rd of September 1952.

92

109
109
14

Facing page, a similarly numerous group Vignale-bodied cars from Maranello featured in another great classic of the 1950s, the Coppa delle Dolomiti.
Top, Paolo Marzotto was victorious with his 225 S in the 1952 edition; another 225 S, driven by Tom Cole and finished in the classic white and blue US racing colours, finished that edition in 7th place overall.

Presented at the Paris Motor Show in October 1953, the Ferrari 250 Europa bodied by Vignale (chassis No. 0295 EU) presented a new colour scheme, with a chrome trim strip running along the flanks, clearly dividing the two colours.

Sinuous and elegant forms, small ovoid air intakes on the flanks, in groups of two or three, slim chrome trim strips dividing the flanks, emphasising the beltline and conspicuous scoops – of extraordinary modernity – near the tail. These were, in short, the styling motifs that became distinguishing features of the Vignale-bodied Ferraris of the 1950s.

The 1953 Mille Miglia was won for the second time by Count Giannino Marzotto in a Ferrari 340 MM Vignale, while the 250 MM Vignale spider No. 544 (chassis No. 0230 MM) driven by director Roberto Rossellini and cameraman Aldo Tonti retired and Sterzi-Rossi 166 MM/53 No. 466 (chassis No, 0278 M) finished 15th overall.

The 1953 Mille Miglia again and more Vignale-bodied Ferrari barchettas and coupés. Tom Cole and Mario Vandelli finished in an excellent 4th place overall in their 340 MM No. 608 (chassis No. 0284 AM).

633

636

Facing page, among the over-2-litre sports cars entered for the 1953 Mille Miglia were the barchettas Nos. 633 and 636 (chassis Nos. 0282 MM and 0274 MM) raced by the Cabianca-Roghi and Scotti-Cattini crews, 9th overall and retired respectively.

With one of the 340 Mexico berlinettas from the 1952 Carrera Panamericana, Eugenio Castellotti also participated in that edition of the Mille Miglia with Ivo Regosa but was unable to finish the race.

ASSICURATRICE UFFICIALE
DELL'AUTOMOBILE
CLUB
XXI°
MILLE MIGLIA
1-2 Maggio
Club
542
542
stelvio

Facing page, evidence of an almost constant presence at the Mille Miglia, in 1954 there were again a number of Vignale-bodied Ferrari at the start: about to start here is No. 542 (chassis No. 0314 M), a 166 MM/53 driven by Primo Pezzoli and Giacomo Moioli "Noris", retired.
The 250 Europa GT from 1954 built on special commission for Princess Liliane de Réthy, the second wife of King Leopold III of Belgium. Alfredo Vignale produced an elegant coupé distinguished by a large panoramic windscreen with reverse-sweep pillars (those of the Chevrolet Corvette were used) and a conspicuous lateral engine bay air vent. The car attracted great attention, thanks in part to the promotional material distributed by the Turin coachbuilder. This was the last Ferrari bodied by Vignale in the golden age of the collaboration with Maranello.

BOSCH
AQUILA
PIRELLI

1954-1957

NOT JUST GTS

THE COACHBUILDER'S OUTPUT WAS NOT EXCLUSIVELY CONFINED TO PRESTIGE SPORTS CARS FOR A VERY WEALTHY CLIENTELE, BUT ALSO TOOK IN MODELS WITH MUCH MORE MODEST MECHANICALS. THIS WAS THE CASE, FOR EXAMPLE, WITH THE BEACH CARS AND THE CUSTOM MODELS BASED ON THE FIAT 600. THE ABARTH 750 GOCCIA CAUSED A SENSATION.

On the facing page, the sensation and futuristic Démon Rouge, penned by Giovanni Michelotti in 1955 and based on Fiat 8V mechanicals.

The thrilling and productive relationship between Vignale and Ferrari came to a close in 1954 with the magnificent 250 Europa GT (chassis No. 0359 GT) built for Princess Liliane de Réthy of Belgium (second wife of King Leopold III) a car that has remained in the annals of the Prancing Horse as one of the greatest examples of formal equilibrium among its two-seater sports cars. These were years of feverish production, during which the renowned Turin coachbuilder, so prolific in terms of new features and so rapidly elevated to the upper reaches of the Italian post-war

The Fiat 1100 Charmant coupé produced by Vignale in a limited series from 1954, based on either the standard version or the TV Turismo Veloce.

coachbuilding school, devoted himself with untiring eclecticism to the production of widely differing vehicle. They included the Alfa Romeo 412 with which Felice Bonetto took 6th place overall in the 1951 Mille Miglia and the Maserati A6 GCS barchetta powered by a 170 hp six-cylinder engine built in 1953 (chassis No. 2049), its long lateral exhausts a highly innovative styling motif. Vignale's creative flair was not restricted to GT cars commissioned by the It crowd of the moment, but was also expressed through a number of modest yet extravagant cars such as the Spiaggia, built in a fair number of examples in 1956 and based on the Fiat 600 Multipla mechanicals. This design did much to stimulate the ephemeral trend for small cars designed to transport holidaymakers in the most fashionable resorts.

And how could we forget the Fiat 1100 Charmant from 1954, an attractive coupé with a sloping tail based on the floorpan of the normal 1100/103 or that of the 1100/103 TV with the 50 hp engine. This was one of the first cars to be produced in a limited series and was followed by numerous others in the late Fifties, many based on the Fiat 600 floorpan, a formula that resulted in the well-known "Vignaline" generation produced in various series with an output that reached up to 40 units per day. This mini-series of small but particularly stylist 600s was enhanced in 1957 by the presentation of Michelotti's futuristic concept car designed around the same platform, the Fiat Abarth 750 Goccia. The first prototype featuring gullwing doors was followed by a second with traditional doors that participated in the very last edition of the Mille Miglia, primarily in order to test the extreme aerodynamics of its compact bodywork in the most demanding of road races. Entrusted to the Luino-Costa crew, the Goccia finished the gruelling event in 94th place overall after having covered the 1,597 kilometres at an average speed of 113 kph.

In 1957, the British Standard-Triumph group turned to Vignale to create the bodywork for its new utility car based on a new mechanical configuration for which a design with a strong personality was required.

A French name – which always adds a touch of elegance – for this model too, again built on Fiat 1100 mechanicals: the Printemps, bodied in 1956 to the designs of Giovanni Michelotti.

The Turin coachbuilder presented the Herald, a unusual car conceived by Michelotti which was launched in 1959-1960 in three versions, saloon, coupé and convertible. The Turin Motor Show of 1958 also saw the presentation of the Triumph Italia 2000 coupé – completely restyled by Michelotti on the TR3 spider chassis – which was then produced by Vignale in a little more than 300 units between 1959 and 1962. The annual sequence of the Turin Motor Show provided a clear overview of the ongoing styling trends and this was the case in 1955 too when the Turin coachbuilder's stand polarized the visitors thronging to admire the provocative red and black bodywork of the Démon Rouge, an extraordinary coupé with lines deliberately swimming against the tide built on the Fiat 8V chassis (1996 cc, 105 hp). This car was particularly memorable thanks to its unusual roof panel cantilevered out over the rear screen and the tail.

The Goccia concept car from 1957 built around Abarth 750 mechanicals (747 cc engine, 43 hp at 5800 rpm) aroused great curiosity. This photo shows the first prototype with gullwing doors; the second prototype, instead fitted with traditional doors, competed in the 1957 Mille Miglia (facing page), entered in the 750 class of the GT category. The original Vignale "vetturette" was driven by Aldo Luino-Mario Costa and finished the race in 94th place overall.

38
228859 • TO

A few moments before the start of the XXII Mille Miglia in 1955 for the Fiat 8V Vignale berlinetta (No. 405) of Vladimiro "Miro" Toselli and Bruno Cavallo who were to retire after having "rounded" the capital.

Alfredo Vignale attracted the attention of the public and the most controversial comments from the specialist press at the 1955 Turin Motor Show with the Démon Rouge, built on a Fiat 8V chassis. It was this provocative creation by Giovanni Michelotti, determined to arouse the curiosity of visitors to the show with a number of extreme features such as the treatment of the upper body with the partially transparent roof panel extended back with a long cantilever over the wrap-around rear screen. Presented with the bodywork finished in a bright red with a black roof, the Démon Rouge hit the spot and was a topic of conversation for many weeks. In 1956 a further two examples were produced, albeit with a less eccentric rook and tail design.

Vignale-Torino
Michelotti
Démon Rouge

BOSCH
AQUILA

342

Facing page, at the 1954 Turin Motor Show Vignale displayed this racing barchetta on an Osca MT4-2AD chassis (1491 cc, 120 hp at 6300 rpm) and then presented at the same show but a year later, the road-going coupé version, bodied on chassis No. 1153. The Osca Mt4 enjoyed great success in competition in that decade. On these pages, "Madero" (Bruno Gavazzoli) and Bruno Franzoni with No. 342 and Giulio Cabianca with No. 343 on the starting ramp for the 1954 Mille Miglia. Of the two, only the second car made it to the finish in 10th place overall.

Michelotti also caused a sensation with the Raggio Azzurro coupé from 1955, built on a tubular chassis by Nardi with mechanical assemblies from the Lancia Aurelia B20. The unusual shape of the windscreen with two transparent Plexiglas domes provoked the most disparate comments. The windscreen was also unusual with a central pillar like that of an aircraft, the circular headlights were inserted into the radiator grille and a two-tone finish was applied, as seen in the photo on the facing page.

Vignale could hardly remain indifferent to one of the most iconic cars of the Fifties, the Giulietta saloon, launched in 1954. The Turin coachbuilder's principal objective was to render that family car "less sober". He achieved this by making recourse to extensive chrome-plating in all areas of the bodywork, underlining and emphasising the various volumes but leaving the underlying composition unchanged.

MICHELIN

In 1955, Vignale once again tackled an Osca, an MT4 1500 coupé built as a one-off and displayed at the Turin Motor Show of that year. Not lacking in interesting features, the car attracted attention thanks to the headlights set into the front grille with two chrome bezels and the deflector set in the middle of the bonnet.

1955 also saw the appearance of this eccentric and extravagant body: a Rolls Royce Silver Wraith commissioned by a New York client who was no less "original" than his car. He asked for and obtain, among other features, comprehensive equipment including a television and a fridge as well as a fully painted engine in an attractive green.

Another car that provided Vignale with a host of ideas was the Fiat 600. Here it is seen in the Nardi 750 (1955) version. The rear-engined layout allowed for a very low, sloping front end which the Turin coachbuilder resolved with a narrow grille and faired headlights. The "panoramico" wrap-around windscreen was also interesting.

In the same period, the Rendez Vous was also based on the 600 Vignale, an elegant coupé that once again had a two-tone livery among its distinguishing features.

The Fiat 1200 (1221 cc engine, 55 hp at 5300 rpm) was taken by Vignale as the basis for the Wonderful coupé, clearly inspired by the fashion for conspicuous tail fins introduced that year on the cars of the Chrysler group; the roof was a removable targa-type rigid panel.

White-wall tyres, a beltline emphasised by a contrasting painted strip, the inevitable tail fins and a rear hatch. These were the stylistic ingredients of the early station wagons from the Fifties. The Garden-car produced by Vignale in 1957 belonged to this extensive family of vehicles.

Lancia launched this convertible model in 1957 (V4 engine, 1089 cc, 53 hp at 4800 rpm) with a wheelbase of 2510 mm. This car became the first model mass produced by Vignale for a major manufacturer and was offered through to 1962.
All the colour photos on these pages have been taken from an official brochure.

TO PROVA

Vignale returned to the Lancia theme for this original Aurelia Blue Ray, built for the Nardi company that used it for developing mechanical assemblies. This fascinating styling exercise appeared in 1957. Two years later it was the turn of the Appia "Lusso" (below), which in this Vignale form confirmed its qualities as a particularly appealing model.

The Alfa Romeo Giulietta in TI form that appeared in 1957 continued to be one of the favourite models for coachbuilders including Vignale who towards the end of the decade produced a series of variants with two-tone paintwork and an emphasis on the already conspicuous tail fins, a "must" in those years.

VIGNALE

1958-1966

GROWTH IMPOSES A NEW FACTORY

THE COMPANY'S RAPID EXPANSION MEANT THAT A NEW FACTORY WAS URGENTLY NEEDED IN ORDER TO MEET THE GROWING DEMAND FROM MANUFACTURERS AND CLIENTS IN ITALY AND ABROAD. HOWEVER, THE SEPARATION FROM MICHELOTTI IN 1962 HERALDED THE BEGINNING OF THE END

The entrance to the new Vignale factory in Strada del Portone No. 80 in Grugliasco to where, in the 1960s, the Turin coachbuilder moved in search of the extra space necessary to satisfy the demands for increased production; sadly, the story was to come to an inglorious end before the decade was out.

In 1957, Vignale started work on its most important commission for a major manufacturer, the Lancia Appia Convertible, a car that immediately highlighted the difficulty in meeting the demands of the market due to the lack of space in the Via Cigliano workshop; to overcome the immediate problems by renting new premises with an area of 400 m^2 in the vicinity on Lungo Dora Voghera, while the firm had to make recourse to a greater number of outside suppliers for the pressing of body panels and in part for painting. However, the situation demanded a more radical solution following the example set by Pinin Farina and Bertone, both of which had moved their production facilities to Grugliasco. Vignale therefore had a new factory built in the same

The Triumph Italia 2000, a slim, elegant coupé once again designed by Michelotti and based on the TR3 A. It was presented at the 1958 Turin Motor Show.

Facing page, presented at the Turin Motor Show of 1959, the Triumph Italia was born out of the Italian importer of the British marque's ambition to propose a combination of the TR3 A spider mechanicals and the bodywork of a typically Italian coupé designed by Michelotti. Attractively styled, the car was not supported commercially by adequate distribution and only 329 examples were produced through to 1962 when the Triumph Motor Company was acquired by Leyland Motors. Above, among the one-offs displayed by Vignale at the Turin Motor show of 1959 there was also this BMW 507 (V8 engine 3165 cc, 150 hp) with hardtop coupé bodywork.

area in Strada del Portone 177, a facility that was inaugurated in the August of 1961 with an initial covered area of 12,000 m^2 and which in any case marked the abandonment of production using the original craft-based techniques in favour of semi-industrial methods.

The demand for prestige cars on the part of the foreign markets and a certain inclination of the Italian clientele towards GT cars with large displacements induced Maserati to enter the field in 1957 with the 3500 GT model. This classic Touring-bodied coupé was flanked at the Geneva Motor Show in 1960 by a spider version, produced by Vignale to the designs of Michelotti and which became one of the most sought-after cars among the young lions of the Sixties. With a wheelbase of 2500 mm (100 mm shorter than the coupé), the Maserati spider boasted irresistible low, sleek lines, free of chrome-plated trim. Powered by the 3.5-litre, twin-cam, straight-six (220 hp), the car boast great roadholding and a maximum speed of over 22 kph. Vignale delivered 250 examples between 1960 and 1964. In 1962, the firm also launched the Maserati Sebring at the

Geneva Motor Show, a coupé built on the short wheelbase of the spider and powered by the same 3.5-litre engine (3485 cc); from 1965, power units with displacements of 3.7 litres (3694 cc) and 4 litres (4014 cc) with power outs of up to 265 hp were available. The Sebring remained in production through to 1968 for a total of 600 examples. Again on behalf of the Trident marque, between 1963 and 1969 the Turin coachbuilder bodied the Quattroporte saloon designed by Pietro Frua. The engine of this last model – a formidable V8 with four overhead camshafts (two per bank) displacing 4.2 litres (later flanked by the 4.7-litre) and a maximum power output of 290 hp (300 for the 4700) – was also fitted to the Mexico coupé bodied by Vignale that made its debut at the Paris Motor Show in 1966 with a semi-monocoque body in steel integrated with a front subframe, and in the four-seater Indy with its rear hatch, of which Vignale built 1,104 examples from 1969 through to 1975.

When the Appia convertible went out of production, Lancia replaced it in 1962 with the new front-wheel drive Flavia model in 2+2 cabriolet form, production of which was again entrusted to Vignale on the basis of a Michelotti drawing, the last produced by the renowned stylist for the Turin coachbuilder.

Designed by Pietro Frua, the Maserati Quattroporte (V8 engine, 4136 cc, 290 hp at 5200 rpm) neatly filled a gap in the range of Italian produced cars; the car featured unitary construction, wheelbase of 2750 mm and a De Dion rear axle. 776 examples were constructed between 1963 and 1969.
Facing page, designed by Virginio Vairo, who had replaced Michelotti at the chief designer at Vignale, the Fiat 850, known in coachbuilding circles as the "Vignalina" (843 cc, 34 hp at 4800 rpm), replaced the 600 D-based model and was offered with three bodywork variants, two-door saloon, coupé and spider.

ASSISTENZA CLIENTI

Michelotti had in fact decided to strike out as a constructor in his own right and had opened a workshop in Via Levanna, from where he was to move to Via Lera and finally to premises in the municipality of Orbassano. This was hardly a consensual separation and while it satisfied the legitimate aspirations of Michelotti it broke up a remarkably effective partnership.

In January 1963, responsibility for styling was entrusted to Virginio Vairo, a new arrival from Pininfarina but one who lacked that exceptional creativity boasted by his predecessor. The interpretative verve of Alfredo Vignale also suffered from that separation. At the Turin Motor Show of 1964, the Turin coachbuilder's stand featured cars built around the mechanicals of the new Fiat 850, while two years later, Vignale bodied for the American Motors group the AMX, an original coupé designed by Richard Teague on a wheelbase of 2460 mm and with a fastback tail and a 5.6-litre V8 engine (280 hp). Teague came up with a novel roof cantilevered over the cockpit and two jump seats in the luggage compartment, a configuration very popular in the America of the Twenties and Thirties. The AMX made its debut on the US market in 1968 and remained in the catalogue for a couple of years.

Bottom, another key moment for Vignale and others was the launch in 1960 of the new Fiat 600 D, used by the Turin coachbuilder as the basis for a series of interesting models in coupé (in the photo), spider and hard top forms. Facing page, the relationship between Vignale and Lancia continued into the new decade with the Flavia Convertible, designed in 1962 by Giovanni Michelotti and produced in more than 1,600 examples.

ALTEX
PIRELLI

Not just Fiat 600s and 850s.
In the second half of the 1950s, Vignale found a source of inspiration in other models from the Turin manufacturer such as the 500 and the 1200.
In the first case, it gave rise to the "Minnie" (facing page top), in the second the "Désirée", bottom, and the "Garden Car", on this page; all models distinguished by sophisticated two-tone paintwork and white-wall tyres.

The prototype Fiat 1500 S coupé from 1959 featured particularly sleek lines that served as the basis for a limited series production model.

Again from 1959, a similarly elegant interpretation of a great BMW classic, the 507 hard top. The wheel covers, like those of the Fiat 1500 on the facing page were interesting and could be defined as "lenticular".

OLLS-ROYCE
ROVER
DE SOTO
TOURING
CHRYSLER
PLYMOUTH
ABARTH & CO.
HUMBER
ABARTH

Facing page, Vignale also displayed a cabriolet prototype based in the Lancia Flaminia (V6, 2485 cc, 119 hp) at the Turin Motor Show in 1959.
Right, the collaboration between Vignale and the British marque Triumph began with the design for the new Herald model for which Michelotti proposed a range of three body styles (saloon, coupé and convertible) with modern but rather un-Italian styling. The car had a separate chassis rather than a monocoque for cost motives. The Herald made its debut at the Royal Albert Hall in London in April 1959.
Below, with the launch in September 1960 of the 600 D (767 cc, 29 hp at 4800 rpm), the popular small Fiat was used by Vignale as the basis for a new generation of customised "Vignalinas" that enjoyed widespread success on the Italian and German markets.

XKV 864

WKV 468

Like the Fiat marque in Italy, on the other side of the Channel it was Triumph, with the Herald model, that provided fertile terrain for the Vignale-Michelotti pairing which proved capable of lending the Herald that touch of "all-Italian" elegance that still today makes it one of the most interesting British cars in both open-top convertible and coupé forms.

The interior and the front end of the Alfa Romeo 2000 2+2 berlinetta presented at the 1960 Turin Motor Show. The front featured rather sharp, angular lines, as seen in the twin headlight units inserted within a chrome bezel. The reinterpretation of the classic Alfa Romeo tri-lobe grille was also rather unsuccessful.

Both from 1962, top, the Fiat 1500 cabriolet with those rectangular headlights that are very evocative of the first Maserati Quattroporte and, below, the Fiat 2300 of just a single example was built.

CEAT

PIRELLI

From the era of the unforgettable Siluro Ricotti, in aerodynamic research the droplet shape has rightly been considered one of the most favourable in terms of the coefficient of aerodynamic penetration. An excellent example of this research was offered by Vignale in 1962 with the 1000 Record Sperimentale, built around Fiat 600 D mechanicals. The front end, upper body – composed of a one-piece glass canopy – and flanks constituted a single enveloping surface. The rear end was instead sharply truncated and characterised by a kind of spoiler integrated into the bodywork.

Sharing the commercial success of the Touring-bodied Maserati 3500 GT coupé (twin-cam straight-six, 3485 cc, 22 hp at 5500 rpm), the Spyder designed by Vignale was presented in 1960 to great acclaim in Italy and abroad. The absence of the roof took nothing away from the beauty of lines that still today make this model one of the great Italian open-top cars. It was also available in a hard top version.

Turin Motor Show, 1963. Another interesting open-top model based on the mechanicals of the Maserati 3500 GTI. The overall composition was particularly elegant, with the narrow, horizontal grille, the soft, sinuous lines of the flanks and the well-modelled tail. Overall it clearly anticipated models such as Pininfarina's Fiat Dino Spider.

44659-GR

The Flavia Convertible (four-cylinder boxer engine, 1500 cc, 92 hp at 5800 rpm), designed by Michelotti and produced from 1962, was a highly desirable car given its full four-seater configuration. The car's well-balanced formal composition is particularly evident in the side view. It was produced in 724 examples through to 1964 and was followed by the 1800 version (102 hp), which remained in production until 1967.

883893 MI

Presented in 1962, the Sebring (straight-six, 3485 cc, 220 hp at 5500 rpm) represented an evolution of the 3500 GT Spyder and was also designed by Giovanni Michelotti. A total of 600 examples were produced through to 1968.
On these pages, the front and rear three-quarters views of the Sebring reveal the absolute elegance and sobriety of the styling, beautifully balanced throughout. In the top photo on this page, two examples at the 1960 Paris Motor Show.

A perfectly preserved
and restored example of
the Maserati Sebring today.

FIAT

Penned by designer Pietro Frua, the Maserati Quattroporte has to be considered as one of the mainstays of the Trident marque. A model of great personality, albeit one not immediately understood in stylistic terms, the Quattroporte from 1963 inaugurated a Maserati tradition that has endured to the present day.

The futuristic New Star Jet prototype built by Vignale for the 1963 Turin Motor Show. An extreme aerodynamic study, it was proposed as a static prototype albeit conceived for a twin-cylinder engine, in the photo.

R-JET

LAMBORGHINI
DAIHATSU
VIGNALE

From the very early Sixties, Vignale began working with Daihatsu which initially commissioned a small compact car with a displacement of just 800 cc. Subsequently, at the 1963 Turin Motor Show, this model served as the basis for an elegant open-top sports car designed by Alfredo Zanellato.

The coupé version of the Daihatsu which maintained sinuous and elegant lines with the unmistakeable front grille and a sloping, close-coupled rear end. Thanks to the extensive glazing the upper body was particularly airy.

Electrolux

Facing page, both the 1500 and the 850 were Fiat models on which Vignale continued to work in the early Sixties. Top, the four-seater 1500 coupé (1963) and below, the 850 cabriolet (1965). On this page, above, the Fiat 1300-1500 cabriolet from 1963 and, below, the Vignale interpretation on the floorpan of the Fiat 600 T van was an updated version of the beach cars.

The Fiat 850 constituted a particular appetising basis for the development of custom models. Virginio Viario and Alfredo Zanellato Vignale were responsible for the 850s with open and closed bodywork produced by Vignale in the mid-Sixties. The open version was particularly successful and well-balanced.

A pure exercise in style, the Fiat 850 Sport coupé, a one-off presented at the 1965 Geneva Motor Show, in two photos of the version slightly modified by Giannini, which appeared at the Turin Show in the same year.

CINTURATO HS

PERSIA
Electrolux
VIGNALE
CINTURATO HS

The particularly sober and well-balanced Fiat 1500 coupé produced by Vignale in 1965, the same year that saw the launch of the Fiat 1300 S, a coupé of a restrained elegance characterised by twin circular headlights set flush with the radiator grille and a beltline characterised by a slight crease.

Alfredo Zanellato Vignale also styled the Opel Kadett A, which first appeared in spider form at the Geneva Motor Show in 1965 and was then presented with closed bodywork at the following Turin Show.

VIGNALE

MORETTI
ITALSUISSE
BIZZARINI
HENRI CHAPRON
OPEL

The Turin Motor Show of 1966 saw Vignale present the Eveline, a sober two-door based around the Fiat 124 mechanicals, with headlights set within chrome bezels similar to those of Maserati Mexico.

Facing page, the Maserati six-cylinder coupé range was updated at the Paris Motor Show of 1966 with the Mexico, equipped with a powerful V8 engine offered with two displacements: 4136 cc (290 hp at 5200 rpm) and 4719 cc (300 hp at 5200 rpm). Instead of the traditional 2+2 accommodation of the sporting coupé, the company opted for a more spacious interior capable of housing four people in comfort. It was produced through to 1972 in 485 examples.

350032 MO

1967-1971
THE RAPID DECLINE AND THE ELEGANT RETURN

IN 1969, CONTROL PASSED INTO THE HANDS OF GHIA AND VIGNALE PERISHED IN A MYSTERIOUS ROAD ACCIDENT. WITH THE ARRIVAL OF FORD THE PRESTIGIOUS NAME GRADUALLY DISAPPEARED. IN 2013, HOWEVER, IT RETURNED TO IDENTIFY AND EXCLUSIVE VERSION OF THE MONDEO; TODAY THE MARQUE IS RESERVED FOR THE FLAGSHIP MODELS IN THE BLUE OVAL'S RANGE.

Facing page, the Gamine, one of the most curious and extravagant models to emerge from the retro trend, designed by Vignale in the second half of the 1960s.
On this page, an official photo of the Fiat 850 Spider, another model in the Vignale catalogue in that period.

Now boasting a workforce of around 200 people, Alfredo Vignale produced the Jensen Interceptor and the FF for the London Motor Show in 1966. This sophisticated car featured four-wheel drive and a V8 Chrysler engine displacing 6.3 litres (330 hp). The following year, the firm also presented the Samantha coupé based on the Fiat 125 and the Gamine, an unusual little open car based on the Fiat 500, the lines of which faithfully reproduced those typical of the two-seater sports cars of the Thirties, inspired by the famous Balilla Coppa d'Oro. Among Vignale's last proposals from 1968 was this controversial station wagon built around Ferrari 330 GT 2+2 mechanicals and the prototype of a flagship saloon, the Tatra 613 powered by a rear-mounted V8.

Alfredo Vignale passed away at the age of 56 in an obscure road accident on the morning of the 16th of November 1969. With him went one of the great craftsmen of Italian coachbuilding, a master sculptor of the contemporary age. As an independent businessman, during a period of little more than 20 years he knew the irresistible euphoria of the artist of exceptional talent, receiving appropriate recognition when, late in 1966, he was awarded the Croce di Commendatore al merito della Repubblica Italiana (Cross of the Knight Commander of the Italian Republic).

The last production model to emerge from the factory was the 1970 Fiat 850 Coupé with four headlights, presented when the company decline was just around the corner, heralded by a drastic cut in daily production (six examples of the Fiat 124 Eveline, around ten Gamines and a Maserati model). Like others in the sector, the company soon had to face up to serious financial difficulties and de Tomaso, which at the time had already taken over the coachbuilder Ghia, with the support of the Ford Motor Company, successfully negotiated the acquisition of the Grugliasco factory. Vignale's last public appearance, at the Turin Motor Show in 1970, was marked by the presentation of a city car, a theme that was already of great interest. In the meantime, de Tomaso formalized the sale of Ghia to the Ford Motor Company, with Vignale also passing into the orbit of the Detroit giant. When Ford gave up the idea of distributing the Pantera as a result of federal regulations that prevent its importation, the Strada del Portone factory was finally closed.

Along with all its assets, the company was sold, while the Vignale marque continued to identify the Ford prototypes presented at the various international motor shows. From 2010, the Ghia name was dropped by Ford, while that of Vignale reappeared at the 2013 Paris Motor Show, distinguishing an exclusive version of the new Mondeo (launched in Europe in 2014), which went into production in 2015. The full Vignale range was presented at the Paris Show in 2016: Mondeo, S-Max, Edge and the Kuga concept car.

Designed by Vairo and assembled around Fiat 500 F mechanicals (air-cooled twin-cylinder engine, 499.5 cc, 18 hp at 4600 rpm), the Gamine flaunted attractive retro styling and was presented as a car for the young at heart. It was launched at the 1967 Paris Motor Show.

VIGNALE

ELECTROLUX
Electrolux

Vignale was responsible for the production of the Touring-designed prototypes and first examples of the British Jensen Interceptor, which made its debut at the London Motor in 1966; in Geneva it was flanked by a prototype two-seater coupé version.

1966, the Eveline, a four-seater coupé based on Fiat 124 mechanicals. The styling was the work of Virginio Vairo.

The Samantha, the car with which Vignale returned to the sports coupé theme, was based on the chassis of the Fiat 125. Below, the collaboration between Vignale and Jensen continued in 1968 with the advent of the Nova model, built on a chassis with a wheelbase shortened by Jensen itself.

The unmistakeable front end of the Samantha, a model produced in 1967 on the basis of the Fiat 125. This angle emphasises the elliptical shape of the headlights that recalled those of the Lamborghini Miura.

The mid-Sixties were marked by an initial veiled interest in "classic cars", a phenomenon that was to explode a couple of decades later. This interest also led to the creation of a number of models with overtly retro styling (take for example the glorious Alfa Romeo 1750 GS of the Thirties, revisited in 1966 with the Gran Sport promoted by *Quattroruote*). The Fiat Gamine was clearly part of this trend (seen on these and the following pages), based on the Fiat 500 F mechanicals and once again designed by Vairo.

VA · 908369

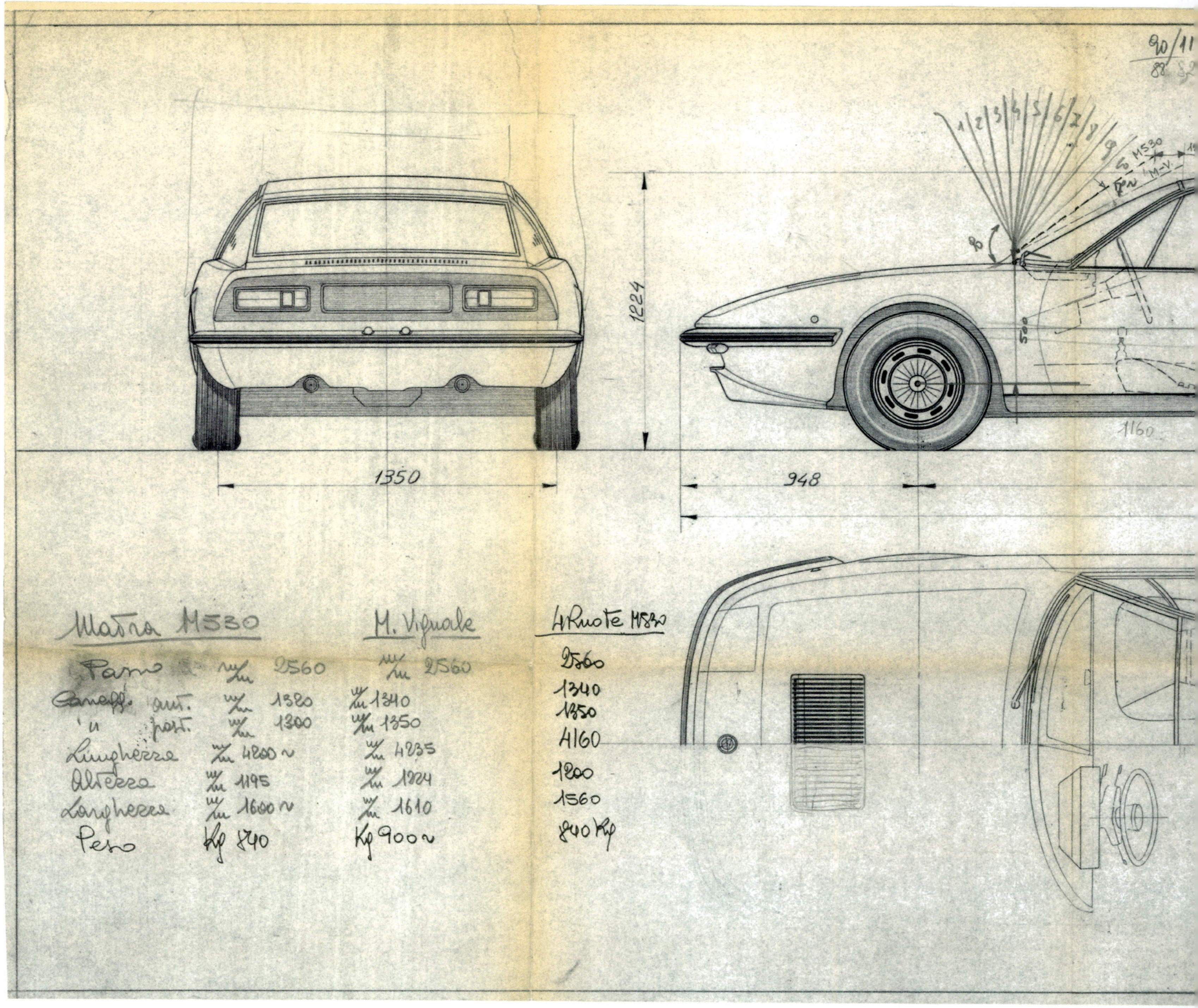
1350
948
1224
1160
Matra M530
M. Vignale
4Ruote M530
Passo m/m 2560
m/m 2560
2560
Carregg. ant. m/m 1320
m/m 1340
1340
" post. m/m 1300
m/m 1350
1350
Lunghezza m/m 4200 ~
m/m 4235
4160
Altezza m/m 1195
m/m 1224
1200
Larghezza m/m 1600 ~
m/m 1610
1560
Peso Kg 840
Kg 900 ~
840 Kg

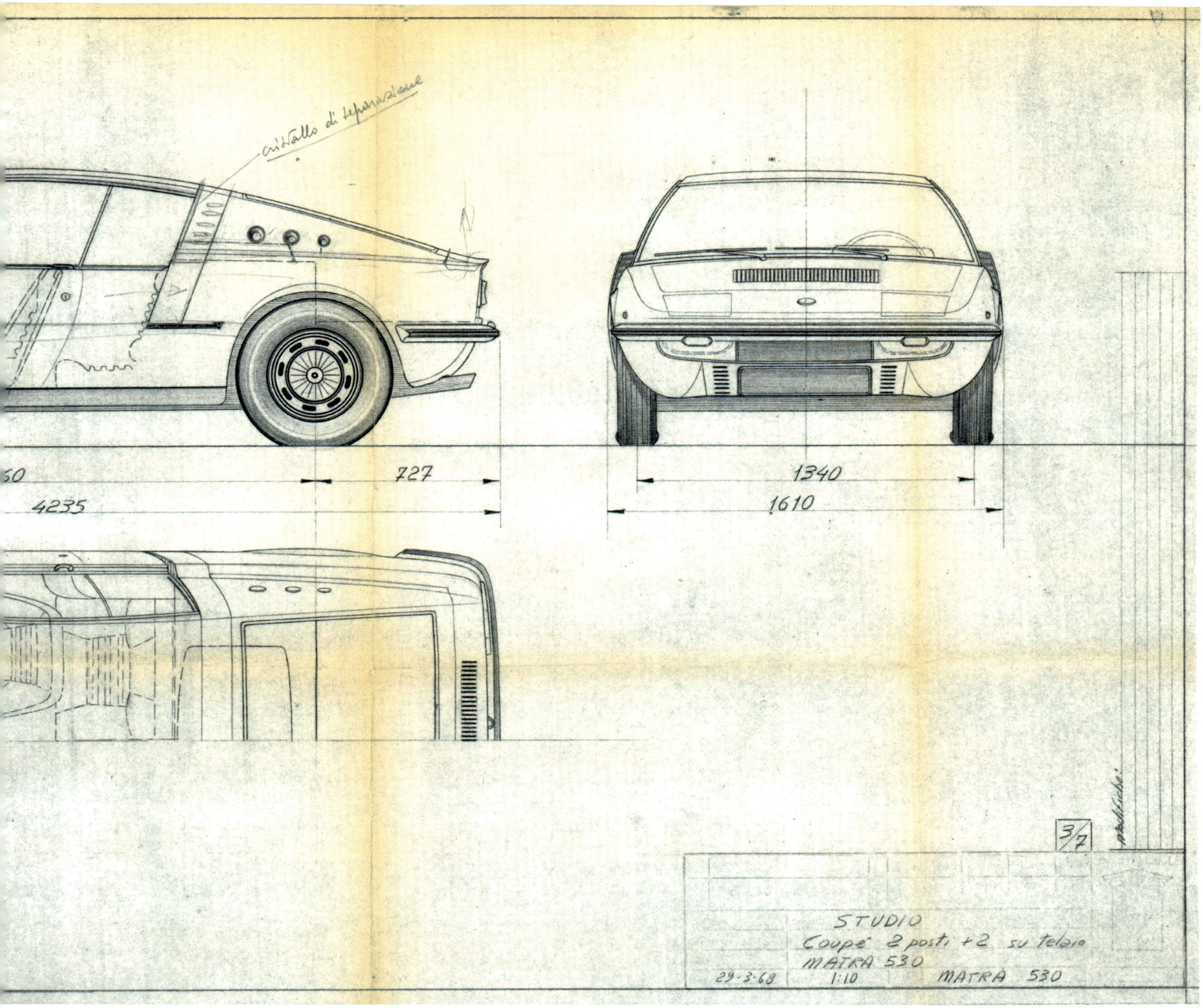

The four dimensioned orthographic views of the Matra M530 coupé, seen in a rare original drawing from the manufacturer. This model appeared at the 1968 Geneva Motor Show.

A number of detail shots of the Matra M 530, an overtly sporting car with a number of features such as the slatted air intakes behind the side windows and the circular cooling vents which referenced the unforgettable Ferrari barchettas and berlinettas of the past.

Vignale displayed this extravagant Ferrari 330 GT on chassis No. 7063 at the Turin Motor Show. It was a station wagon designed by Bob Peak on behalf of Luigi Chinetti Jr. The sacrilegious car attracted the most bitter criticism.

The styling of the 613, a large flagship saloon for the Czech firm Tatra, represented the last major project by Alfredo Vignale who developed an initial styling prototype in 1969 based on a rolling chassis with sophisticated mechanicals (a rear-mounted, air-cooled V8 engine with four overhead camshafts, 3495 cc, 165 hp at 5200 rpm), with clear references to the models from the late Thirties designed by Hans Ledwinka. The 613 remained in production from 1974 through to 1996.

Previewed at the Turin Motor Show in 1968, the Maserati Indy (seen here) represented the two-box evolution of the classic Mexico model. Thanks to the adoption of pop-up headlights, the car boasted a very low and sleek front end. Vignale assembled 1,104 units between 1969 and 1975.

A low, sloping front end, pop-up headlights, an airy upper body with extensive glazing, a sharp crease along the beltline and a truncated tail. The Indy, a masterpiece and one of the most iconic Maseratis of all time.

The assembly lines and a number of stages in the assembly of the De Tomaso Pantera in Carrozzeria Vignale's strada del Portone factory in the early Seventies.

The De Tomaso Pantera in all its angular beauty, with its taut and evocatively dynamic lines.

The last four pages of this book offer an over view of the post-Vignale Vignale, when the marque changed hands a number of times, from De Tomaso to Ghia before being absorbed along with this other historic Italian coachbuilding name, by Ford, which was to use the Vignale name to identify models of particular prestige. Among the first models of this new era was the Ford Mustang Vignale, which was actually built by Ghia and appeared at the Turin Motor Show in 1984.

The Aston Martin Lagonda Vignale concept car built by Ghia in 1993.

From the top, clockwise: the Lincoln Vignale, a styling study for a flagship cabriolet from 1987; the Ford TSX-4 Vignale, a design for a high-tech station wagon from 1984; the Ford Focus Vignale, a coupé-cabriolet from 2004.

VIGNALE

In recent years the Vignale marque has been used to lend prestige to a number of prototypes built by Ghia to designs from the Detroit manufacturer, including the S-Max from 2014, on this page right, and the Ford Mondeo (in the other photos), which appeared in 2013 and went into production in 2015 in the Valencia factory in Spain.

Printed by
D'Auria Printing - Ascoli Piceno
(Italy)
September 2019

masterpieces of style

pieces of style masterpieces of style m
pieces of style masterpieces of style m
pieces of style masterpieces of style m
pieces of style masterpieces of style m
pieces of style masterpieces of style m
pieces of style masterpieces of style m
pieces of style masterpieces of style m
pieces of style masterpieces of style m
pieces of style masterpieces of style m
pieces of style masterpieces of style m
pieces of style masterpieces of style m
pieces of style masterpieces of style m
pieces of style masterpieces of style m